KU-783-172

Little People, **BIG DREAMS**

FRIDA KAHLO

Written by
Mª Isabel Sánchez Vegara

Illustrated by
Gee Fan Eng

Translated by Emma Martinez

Frances Lincoln
Children's Books

Frida Kahlo was born in Mexico. Just by looking at her you could see she was special.

When she was at school she got really sick.

The illness made her leg as skinny as a rake.

But Frida didn't complain. She was different. She liked to dress differently, too.

Then one day, a bus Frida was riding crashed into a car. Life as she knew it changed forever.

After her accident, Frida had to rest in bed.
To help the hours pass, she drew pictures
of her foot.

Then, even though she was still in pain, Frida decided to draw self-portraits using a mirror.

Painting by painting, Frida – and her art – got better. It was time to show her pictures to someone else.

She visited the famous artist, Diego Rivera, who couldn't believe his eyes. He wasn't sure what he liked more – her pictures, or her.

Frida and Diego fell in love. They were so similar,
and yet so different. But through their ups and downs,
Diego encouraged Frida in her paintings.

Through her wonderful pictures, Frida spoke about how she was feeling. In some she looked sad but in others, she smiled.

Eventually Frida decided to show everyone her work.
Her pictures caused a great stir in New York City.

When the exhibition came to Mexico, Frida was so ill she had to be in bed. But it was clear that nothing could stop her from painting – not illness, pain or heartache.

Frida Kahlo taught the world to wave goodbye to bad things and say "Viva la vida"...

"Live life."

FRIDA KAHLO

(Born 1907 • Died 1954)

1919

1939

Frida Kahlo was born in Coyoacán, a small town outside of
Mexico City. When she was six, she contracted polio, leaving
one leg skinnier than the other. As she grew older, she took part
in tomboy activities like riding a bike and playing sports, and
once wore male clothes and slicked back her hair for a family
photograph. In 1925, Frida was in a bus crash that left her with
a lot of painful injuries, including a broken collarbone, ribs and
pelvis. While recovering, instead of continuing her studies, she
took up painting – mainly pictures of herself – from her bed.

1942–5   1944

Her husband, the famous Mexican artist Diego Rivera, was
a great supporter of her artwork, and in 1938 Frida had her
first solo exhibition in New York City. However, Frida only
became famous internationally after her death. Her paintings
are instantly recognisable because of their bright colours and
symbols of Mexican culture, and have been sold for millions
of pounds around the world. Thanks to her strong personality,
fighting spirit and love of painting, Frida overcame the accident
that marked her life. She is an inspiration to many women today.

Want to find out more about **Frida Kahlo**?

Have a read of these great books:

Who Was Frida Kahlo? by Sarah Fabiny and Jerry Hoare

Frida and Diego: Art, Love and Life by Catherine Reef

13 Women Artists Children Should Know by Bettina Shuemann

And if you're in Mexico City, you could even visit the house that Frida lived in!

www.museofridakahlo.org.mx

Quarto is the authority on a wide range of topics.
Quarto educates, entertains and enriches the lives of
our readers—enthusiasts and lovers of hands-on living.
www.quartoknows.com

First published in the UK in 2016 by Frances Lincoln Children's Books,
74–77 White Lion Street, London N1 9PF, UK
QuartoKnows.com
Visit our blogs at QuartoKnows.com

© 2014 by Frida Kahlo Corporation (or FK) All Rights Reserved.
Text copyright © 2014 by Mª Isabel Sánchez Vegara
Illustrations copyright © 2014 by Gee Fan Eng

First published in Spain in 2014 under the title *Pequeña & Grande Frida Kahlo*
by Alba Editorial, s.l.u.
Baixada de Sant Miquel, 1, 08002 Barcelona
www.albaeditorial.es

All rights reserved.

Translation rights arranged by IMC Agència Literària, SL

No part of this publication may be reproduced, stored in a retrieval system, or transmitted, in any form,
or by any means, electrical, mechanical, photocopying, recording or otherwise without the prior written permission
of the publisher or a licence permitting restricted copying. In the United Kingdom such licences are issued by the
Copyright Licensing Agency, Barnard's Inn, 86 Fetter Lane, London, EC4A 1EN.

A catalogue record for this book is available from the British Library.

ISBN 978-1-84780-770-0

Printed in China

9 8

Photographic acknowledgements (pages 28-29, from left to right) 1. Photo © FineArt / Alamy 2. Diego Rivera with Wife Frida
Kahlo, Photo © Bettmann/CORBIS 3. Frida Kahlo reclining on her bed in Coyoacán, Mexico, between 1942 and 1945, Chester
Dale papers, 1897-1971, (bulk 1950-1968), Photo © Archives of American Art, Smithsonian Institution 4. Frida Kahlo © Corbis

Also in the *Little People,* **BIG DREAMS** series:

COCO CHANEL

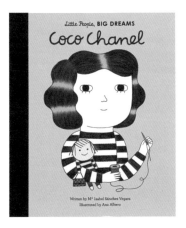

ISBN: 978-1-84780-771-7

Following the death of her mother, Coco Chanel spent her early life in an orphanage, where she was taught how to use a needle and thread. From there, she became a cabaret singer, seamstress, hat-maker and, eventually, one of the most famous fashion designers that has ever lived. The inspiring story of this international style icon features a facts and photos section at the back.

Discover the lives of outstanding people, from designers and artists to scientists. All of them achieved incredible things, yet each began life as a child with a dream.